PUTIN'S NEW
WORLD ORDER

PUTIN'S NEW WORLD ORDER

JOHN BURNHAM

DEDICATED
TO THE PEOPLE
OF RUSSIA WHO
HAVE SUFFERED
CENTURIES OF
CORRUPT AND
OPPRESSIVE
RULE

CONTENTS

INTRODUCTION

For some time now Mr. Putin has been trying to ridicule US exceptionalism, complaining that the US is imposing its will and morals around the world.

Presumably Mr. Putin feels insulted that Russia, his great country, is being somehow belittled by foreign ideas and morality. It is vital to understand why this is important: the US — a foreigner — is giving ideas to Russians!

Russia has always been suspicious of foreigners throughout her history.

Totally by-passed by the Renaissance, and beholden to an ultra-conservative religion, Russia has always treated non-Russians with disdain. Including those whose lands were colonized and taken over by Russia over the centuries.

It was OK for Catherine the Great (herself a foreigner) and Peter the Great to import foreigners to work in Russia, and it is OK for BP, Exxon and ENI to develop Russia's oil sector. But it is not OK to bring in foreign morality and ideas. Russia is closed to foreign ideas, especially the idea of free speech and free expression, the rights to assemble and protest, and indeed human rights in general. According to Mr. Putin these rights are exceptional in the West only, not in Russia. These rights are foreign to his thinking.

While ridiculing US exceptionalism, Mr. Putin is of course claiming Russian exceptionalism, Russian greatness. But is anyone listening? It is not what one person wants to be — it is what the rest think of him. The US may claim exceptionalism but it is up to the world to decide whether that's true.

The same with Russian exceptionalism (or Chinese or French).

Within Mr. Putin's years in power, China became an economic superpower with a vast infrastructure of highways, bullet trains and great new cities as well as a home-grown export industry. Hosted an Olympics, too. The French still produce over 1000 cheeses (with a little help from the EU). What has Mr. Putin achieved — the Sochi Olympics? Great! Magnificent! Well done! But what else? Where are the roads, the hospitals and badly needed new housing. Where did all the oil and gas billions go?

The Soviet Union collapsed as a result of exceptional corruption and mismanagement. Has anything changed since then? Who in Russia's government has exceptional management skills and how and when is Russia going to prosper? If US ideas are not welcome, how about learning something from China? That truly is a success story that can apply to Russia, if Mr. Putin wants to learn something from others.

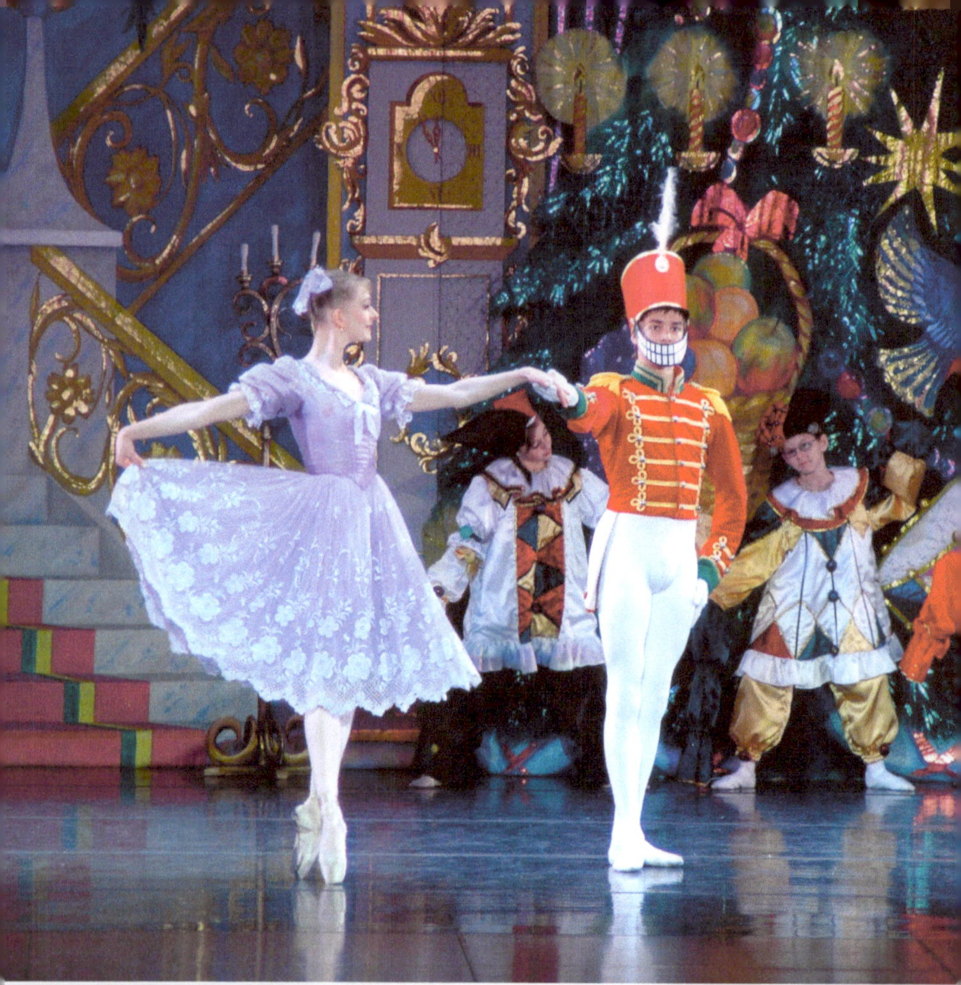

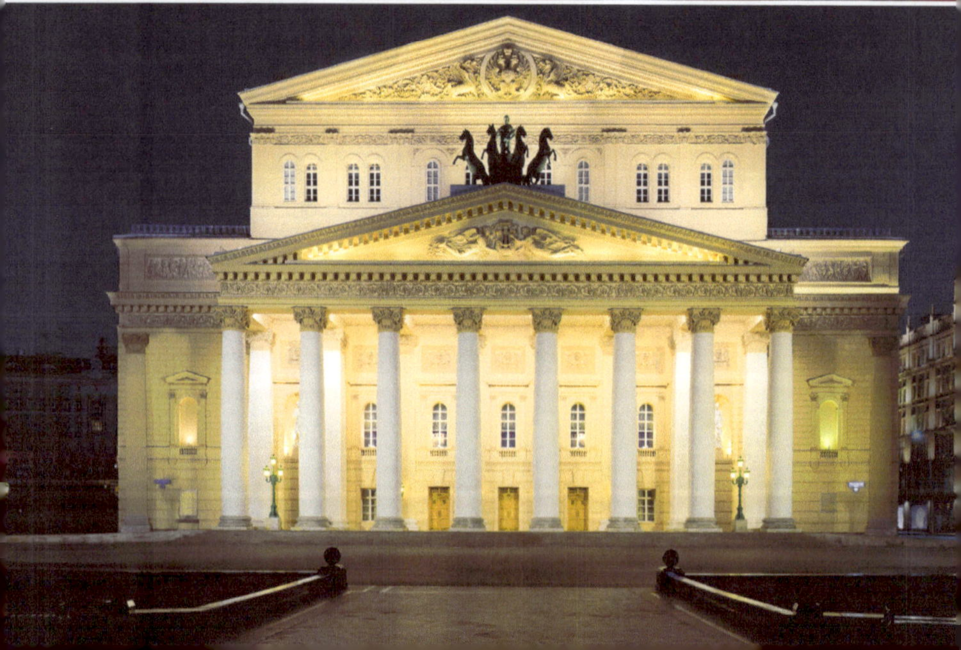

The Good

Have you ever seen "The Nutcracker"?

In the first row of the Bolshoi theater!?

At Christmas?!

You can't beat that. Nobody can. It's magic! and it is exceptional!

Russia is exceptionally good in the arts, the classical arts especially. Most of Russia's great artists lived and worked before Soviet rule, and very little was created during Soviet times. However, despite repression of ideas and human rights, despite a ban on foreign travel, despite KGB control of everyday life, some great works were created in the Soviet era and some great artists did emerge, at a cost of exile, prison and persecution of the entire family.

One has to admire the exceptional ability of the Russian people to endure hardship — whether under serfdom under the czars, as starving proletarians during Soviet communism, or, as now, under Putin's repression of expression and human rights.

It seems Russian exceptionalism can be summed up in one word: endurance.

Russia survived invasions by the Mongols, Swedes and Germans, as well as its own Stalinist purges. All this followed by 75 years of Soviet corruption and mismanagement.

Has Mr. Putin changed anything? Did he eliminate corruption? Has he improved management of the economy? What has he done to prevent another collapse?

There are only two countries in the world where the people are very similar in their world outlook — Russia and the US. When you talk to the average Russian or American one immediately gets the feeling that these people belong to a vast country, they are never small-minded and are rather generous. The average Russian is much like the average American.

But there are also deep differences between the two.

A Russian never whistles indoors . . . it is bad luck.

A Russian never shakes hands through an open door. Also bad luck.

The country is full of superstitions and unwritten do's and don'ts . . .

Where the American looks always ahead the Russian always carries the past.

Where an American would greet a stranger in the street the Russian may turn hostile. Suspicion is everywhere.

Thanks to the legacy of Stalin and the KGB. Being suspicious of strangers is a mode of self-preservation.

Russia has everything—vast territory (12 time zones), alpine mountains, oceans and seas, lakes and rivers. And minerals! From oil and gas to gold and aluminum. And caviar, too.

Theoretically it can be the richest nation on earth! And it should be.

Why it is not is because, other than Yeltsin and Gorbatchov, nobody ever admitted past mistakes, nobody ever wanted to learn from past failures, while the country continues to be mismanaged in the same old fashion as the Soviet Union before that. Instead of looking ahead and let go of the terrible past, Mr. Putin wants to recreate the old Soviet Union. What didn't work for 75 years must work now.

Mr. Putin says so.

Like the Soviet Union, the Ukraine was ruled by an exceptionally corrupt inner circle, led by Yanukovich. He was finally thrown out and, if the Ukraine is to survive as an independent nation, the new rulers must clean house and bring in competent management, even if it is foreign. A good lesson for Russia, one would assume.

Yes, Russia has the potential to be a truly great nation if she is willing to embrace the world and not treat it with suspicion. Be a partner and not an adversary. There are many gifted and successful Russians around the world—sportsmen, businessmen, artists. Just think of Maria Sharapova

and Gergiev, the opera director or Anna Netrebko, the soprano: all of them had the benefit of access to foreign ideas in addition to being loyal Russian citizens.

These are the names and faces that people around the world admire — they are Russia's most valuable assets. But imagine how many more assets Russia would gain if Mr. Putin opened the lid on freedom of expression and new ideas, not necessarily of foreign origin!

"They asked for ice cream,

he delivered Crimea"

The BAD

Lenin, Stalin and Putin are also famous. The first two made sure to destroy private ownership of almost everything from agriculture to industry via theft (nationalization) of property and replacing the owners and experts with "proletarians," i.e. incompetent corrupt apparatchiks who mismanaged the economy for 75 years.

Even worse, free thinking (any thinking) was forbidden for the duration of Soviet rule. The result is total apathy, indifference, lack of initiative –why bother to say, think or invent anything if you are going to be punished for it? "Shut up! Don't think!" (Molchat! ne rassuzhdat!) is expected.

Mr. Putin continues the intellectual oppression started by his illustrious predecessors. So how is he going to create a Great Russia when no one dares to initiate anything and everyone is scared and waiting for their leader to say what needs to be done, how, when and where it needs to be done. He always knows best.

He has stated that he wants Russia to be great again, to be reckoned with, to be feared. The Crimea invasion achieved the fear factor instantly but what now? When will Russia produce something other than fear that will impress the world? Something "Made in Russia" that everyone admires. And why would you want to scare your neighbors?

They should be your best customers!

While Russia still exports Stolichnaya vodka China has flooded the world with everything from toys to clothing to electronics and cars "Made in China" as have many developing nations in Asia. How great can a country be if it only produces vodka? Oil and gas are a gift from nature so Mr. Putin can't claim these as his achievements.

There's something very wrong with Russia's inability to deal with its economy and environment. Instead of working with its neighbors as partners for mutual benefit Russia is always using blackmail to subdue them and impose its will. Always adversarial it blocks wine and mineral water exports from tiny Georgia, blocks Moldovan wine to the Russian market and Ukrainian goods of any type to cross the border.

Why? Just because their governments dare to think of being friends with both Russia and the EU? Why does Russia use blackmail instead of compromise? War instead of trade?

The answer lies with Mr. Putin and his predecessors.

The main mistake people make about Russia is that they all assume Russia should behave like the rest of Europe or the US. What people don't realize is that Russia economically, socially and politically is like the US in 1910!

Initial accumulation of capital, oligarchs with no social conscience, predatory behavior. No infrastructure in the country; mud, soot and awful work environment. Rampant poverty, with only some social services and only in the main cities.

The fact that Russia put a man in space and has nuclear weapons doesn't make her an advanced, rich country. Russia is still a third world country, with nuclear weapons. Lots of them. Like North Korea: starving the population but terrorizing everyone around, including advanced countries like Japan and South Korea.

Why is the 1910 comparison important?

Because a hungry person can only think of food. Then a roof over his head. Then family and a bigger space. Then a car, then a dacha, then a foreign trip: only then, possibly, will this person start thinking of interacting with others (his neighbors) in a friendlier fashion.

Russia is at the initial stage of finding food for all but has not yet managed to secure a roof for all its population:

the housing stock, even in major cities, dates from the 19th century — dilapidated, decrepit, uncomfortable.

It is even worse in the countryside.

Many Russians already have cars and many do have dachas but getting there is a big problem. There is no infrastructure and the bad roads are littered with broken-down trucks and cars, with very (very!) few service stations along the roads. Tesla's electric cars will never make it here.

The average time for a taxi ride from central Moscow to Sheremetyevo airport is easily over two hours, sometimes over three and four hours! One way.

Importantly, due to the horrible traffic jams, the Moscow rich, including most in Mr. Putin's cabinet, have to travel for over two hours sometimes to get to their dachas in Rublyovka, a posh weekend village just 30 miles away.

But don't worry, when Mr. Putin's motorcade comes they close the road for an hour before he gets there — let the masses sit and wait in their cars.

Yes, you need exceptional endurance to live in Russia. How can you be friendly after sitting in a car for hours? These daily inconveniences drain people's energy to smile or enjoy themselves after work. If they do they do it recklessly — alcoholism and cigarettes are the main reasons behind the dangerously low life-expectancy rates for men in Russia, 55 years.

Russia has a long way to go before it becomes a smiling friendly neighbor.

Mr. Putin's main concern should be rebuilding housing, developing road and rail infrastructure, communications in the country outside the big cities. Instead he spent a fantastic sum of $53 billion on the Olympics. Successful, no doubt, but imagine how many miles of road this could have yielded!

The Sochi Olympics were meant to show the world what Russia is and what she can achieve if given the opportunity to think and create freely.

It was a magnificent display of creativity and imagination at its best, and the goodwill created should have lasted for years.

But it was wasted as soon as Russia invaded Crimea.

And then everything changed.

People forgot the Olympics and looked in disbelief at TV images of Russian troops "liberating" another country against its will. The subsequent farce with the referendum and annexation totally negated the Olympic goodwill.

A total waste of $53 Billion!

Did anyone in Russia question Mr. Putin's decision? How can any country on earth afford to waste $53 billion, especially a poor country such as Russia? How can the risk of becoming a pariah state justify such decision?

The invasion of Crimea changed the world in an instant. Totally unprovoked invasion of a sovereign country took place in the 21st century, 25 years after the end of Cold War One.

What comes next is on everyone's mind. But whatever it is it is going to be bad before it gets better.

Especially for Russia.

What is Russia's gain? What kind of calculation justifies all this?

Going back to the collapse of the Soviet Union: in addition to exceptional corruption and mismanagement there was one more reason for the collapse — the unstable, reckless and inefficient workforce.

"We pretend to work and they pretend to pay us," was the joke in Soviet days. It is still valid.

Russia's workforce, especially men, are frequently drunk or missing after nights out, and many are not suited to the jobs they have. Theft of industrial or private property is rampant; crime is high.

In addition to low pay, people have to deal with corrupt low-level administrators everywhere. Protection rackets are proliferating.

Traffic police are famous for taking bribes and issuing tickets for no reason (unless they get a bribe).

Daily life in Russia is tough. Very tough. Few people smile, more people drink, many are killed in car accidents or by vodka and cigarettes. The Russian diet is famously lacking fresh fruit and vegetables. It is a meat and potatoes diet and, of course, cucumbers! Good with vodka.

In short, Russia needs time to:

satisfy its huge basic needs

obtain self-confidence

start smiling

start behaving as a good neighbor

be accepted as a good neighbor

. . . getting out of Crimea would be a good start.

The Ominous

(KGB State)

IN THE YELTSIN DAYS OF ANARCHY, oligarchs and hyperinflation, everyone was hoping that Russia might get a tough, honest and competent leader who would eliminate corruption, restore order and prosperity to the country. People were hoping for a strong and straightforward person, who would stabilize the country and introduce democracy. Someone who didn't belong to the Soviet Nomenklatura but had the status and experience to deal with the Soviet legacy.

President Yeltsin picked Mr. Putin to succeed him — a man with a KGB background who would clean Russia of corruption, restore order and bring prosperity. He was the tough guy everyone had hoped for. But was he the right tough guy?

Mr. Putin quickly reined in the oligarchs by putting one of them in jail for daring to enter politics and question his policies. True to his background, Mr. Putin never took criticism lightly: dissent and demonstrations were not tolerated and protesters and opposition leaders were harassed and jailed.

The KGB's main focus and goal during Soviet days was to restrain opposition by suppressing any form of criticism of government policies.

Mr. Putin's style is still the same KGB mindset — the state controls the media totally, and any demonstration against the government is considered criminal. In short, Mr. Putin has not changed a bit by becoming a president and continues ruling according to the KGB book. "Once a KGB agent — always a KGB agent," as the saying goes.

Mr. Putin is surrounded by former KGB agents who now run the country (and prosper themselves). Why is this bad? Because by nature, schooling and experience these people are not open minded, are not rational and are highly unpredictable. They want to impose their will, their way, without compromise, on all occasions. This is especially critical for Russia's dealings with the rest of the world. For Mr. Putin and his KGB "siloviki" team do not care what the world thinks of his decisions, and that makes Russia a very dangerous player — like North Korea, only more dangerous.

The European Union is built on the principles of compromise and goodwill. So how can they negotiate with an irrational and unpredictable Russia? Especially with a man who doesn't know the meaning of compromise? Someone who wants everything done HIS way!? One must remember that Stalin once signed a non-aggression treaty with Hitler. Was that rational? Who was his advisor? The KGB.

Mr. Putin has already proved he doesn't care about world opinion by invading Georgia in 2010, during the China Olympics. By invading Crimea he has confirmed, once again, that Russia doesn't follow international rules of conduct, doesn't accept international laws and is willing to dare anyone for a fight.

Mr. Putin is spoiling for a fight: his attitude is "come and fight me if you dare!" This is his idea of building a Greater Russia.

Obviously becoming a pariah state has not entered his calculations, nor is anyone able to question him at home.

Some are trying to excuse his actions with his complaints about being slighted by the West over the years. Is invasion the best cure? Is this invasion the last, or is there another one coming at the next Olympics?

Can any murderer be excused for committing a crime to teach someone a lesson? A crime is a crime and there is no need to prove guilt after invasion.

Maybe the better explanation for these invasions is Mr. Putin's inability to bring prosperity to Russia. The economy is stagnating, mismanagement and corruption are rampant. So these "little" invasions are diverting tactics so the people at home will feel great. The Sochi Olympics, too, were a diversion.

In short, Mr. Putin is fighting for his own political life, while at the same time tarnishing the image of his country as he continues his rule. And, just like President Lukashenko, it seems that Mr.Putin too will "sacrifice" himself and rule for life.

Mr. Putin has now become the world's worst nightmare — an unpredictable, unstable ruler with a huge nuclear arsenal. True to his background and goals of establishing a Greater Russia, he is totally capable of blackmailing neighbors into submission. Armenia has already agreed to abstain from joining the EU, while Kazakhstan and Belarus have already joined Putin's customs union as a step towards the envisaged Eurasian Union. But what happened to the Commonwealth of Independent States? Did nobody join?

Dealing with Putin

The European Union should be very grateful to Mr. Putin for one thing—his actions in Crimea will force the EU to finally set up a Common Defense Policy in addition to their Common Foreign Policy. All EU countries have been freeloading on defense, happily purring under the US protective umbrella. This is no longer enough, and all EU countries should start to contribute towards a common defense by increasing their military budgets and acting in united fashion in the face of a common threat.

Germany should lead this time despite pacifist cries at home. As the biggest EU investor in Russia, Germany has the most to lose if it allows Mr. Putin to continue destabilizing Eastern Europe.

The US, too, must up its game in Eastern Europe and the Ukraine by resurrecting intelligence operations and facilities, including cyber-intelligence.

In true KGB style Mr. Putin has started publishing embarrassing taped conversations between EU and US officials. Should the West respond with similar actions? Surely, there must be embarrassing moments in a man's life.

Mr.Putin will not change his expansionist strategy unless tough sanctions are imposed. He doesn't understand diplomacy and doesn't care about it.

There should be no meetings unless Russia pulls back from Crimea, its forces pull back from the Ukrainian border and Mr.Putin submits his proposal in writing. Any other meetings will be useless smokescreens. Why meet someone who uses provocation and blackmail to start negotiations? That would be endorsing blackmail.

Name and Shame

The Ukraine should take Russia to court for breaking her pledge to protect Ukraine's sovereignty. The Ukraine should demand compensation for all investment lost as well as the territory itself — a huge piece of valuable real estate. It can bring billions to the Ukraine while getting rid of a budget drain. Let Putin choke on it!

The OSCE should take Russia to court for violating OSCE's treaties about post WWII borders.

The UN Security Council should publicly denounce Russia for its actions and demand withdrawal from the Crimea. If it doesn't, it should be denied membership of the Security Council. Russia's invasion of the Crimea renders its membership of the Security Council a farce!

It's time to reveal publicly Mr. Putin's holdings and those of the "siloviki".

It's also time to reveal publicly Mr. Putin's mismanagement of the economy on a scale that may yet lead to another Soviet-style collapse.

It's time to work closely with Kazakhstan against a possible repetition of the Crimea "liberation" action.

And it's definitely time to make sure the next Olympic games will not be associated with yet another Putin invasion!

Next on the UN Agenda: suspend Russia from the Security Council

Russia's invasion of the Crimea has changed the post-WWII world order.

No doubt the rules have to be changed to foresee future actions by rogue governments, especially such with nuclear weapons.

Russia's membership in the UN Security Council is now a farce and belittles this UN body.

Russia should be suspended from the Security Council until she pulls out of Crimea.

AFTERWORD

Reasons to be cheerful

It's not all bad and we should be grateful to Mr. Putin for making a huge mistake by invading Crimea. Let go of the past and look to the future!

The Ukraine should be grateful to Russia for uniting the Ukrainian population in its pursuit of closer relations with the EU. If the Ukrainian people get rid of corruption and establish a competent, technocratic regime, the country should have a bright future with help of the IMF, US and the EU.

The EU should be grateful to Russia for Mr. Putin's wake-up call as a spur to finally setting up its Common Defense Policy as well as increasing its member states' long-neglected military budgets.

NATO should be grateful for getting a meaningful objective: protecting its members from an unpredictable and reckless neighbor.

The US should be grateful for having a newly alerted EU ally who will finally share the burden of its own defense.

In all, Mr. Putin has done everyone a favor, except for Russia.

www.ingramcontent.com/pod-product-compliance
Lightning Source LLC
Chambersburg PA
CBHW050843290526
45792CB00002B/503